I0772506

The New Rules of Sex Workbook

A step-by-step guide to re-writing the rules
of your sex and love life

Dr. Lauren Brim

Table of Contents

Introduction

"Our beliefs control our bodies, our minds,
and thus our lives."
- Bruce H. Lipton, *The Biology of Belief*

Welcome. Whether you have just finished reading *The New Rules of Sex*, are doing this workbook simultaneously, or are doing it alone, I am so pleased that you have found your way here! I wanted to begin by welcoming you to the journey of rethinking your sexual paradigm and starting the process of discovering who you truly are as a sexual being (and the happiness that is found along the way). The way we raise our children in society funnels them into a sexual and relationship model that is rarely questioned. The current paradigm has been: date one person at a time, abstain from sex until commitment or marriage, and then enter into monogamous marriage with that partner for the rest of your life. Does that sound familiar? And that is only the beginning. There are rules and taboos that govern masturbation, sexual positions and activities, sexual education, same-sex attraction, fetishes, unequal libido in partnerships, whether we talk about sex with friends, if we have sex during pregnancy and childrearing, and the list goes on and on. I created this workbook because these ideas about sex are very limiting to ourselves and our relationships, and this method of self-examination will help you to break down your belief systems and education around sex and apply what you learned in *The New Rules of Sex* to create a more satisfying life. Even those who have not read the book can benefit from the journey they take in this workbook to unravel the rules and beliefs they have about sex and discover more of who they truly are as empowered sexual beings.

I was raised to fall in love with the opposite sex, date monogamously with the goal of marriage, and hold back the expression of my sexuality until that marriage was entered into for life. I had a lot of fear of going against that model because it was also connected to the religion I was raised with and the concepts of sin, punishment, shame and guilt that accompanied noncompliance. It was only just before my thirtieth birthday that I began to challenge what I was raised to believe and what I continued to hear through some of the most popular sex and relationship coaches of the time. A woman hadn't found a husband because she was sleeping with her ex-boyfriend? Or because she slept with men too soon? Why were women still required to resist the sexual advances of men to prove their value as women? Coaches were still preaching that the ultimate goal for women was marriage where they would leave the horrible realm of dating and live happily-ever-after in marital bliss, but was that narrative really true? Before I was able to challenge such powerful ideas around sexuality and relationships, I first had to hit rock bottom and go through my own dark night of the soul, spending tens of thousands of dollars on a dating coach, only to end up heartbroken and more lost and depressed than I had ever been in my life. It was at that point I began to research what was really true about human sexuality, and I shared that research along with my own stories of sexuality in *The New Rules of Sex*.

So, let's get started examining who we are as sexual beings beneath the education, belief systems, and inherited shame from our families and culture. I am positive that you will find yourself more liberated, happy, and turned on by life than you ever thought possible at the completion of this journey. And you deserve it! Let's dive in.

Chapter 1: Where do you come from?

In this first chapter we will start to explore what you have learned about sexuality from your family and the town or city where you were raised. There are so many subtle things that are communicated to us by our parents, grandparents and the community that surrounds us. It's not just what they say, but what they don't say, how their bodies and voices tighten or relax, the way their faces respond, and the comments that are made in a instant that can affect the entire course of our sex lives. Their relationship to pleasure, sexuality, bodies and relationships are all passed down to us both consciously and unconsciously unless we take the time to question them. Scientists have found that we also genetically inherit the effects of the environment and life experiences on the genes of our parents, grandparents, and even great-grandparents. Trauma, such as sexual abuse, sexual shaming, or a difficult pregnancy or childbirth, can be passed down to offspring through inherited DNA in what are called epigenetic changes. This is why we cannot begin to look at our sexuality until we uncover what we have inherited from our ancestors. What were the lives of our grandparents like? What was our parent's relationship to sexuality? What did your mother endure while she was pregnant with you or while you were a very small child? All of these messages and epigenetic factors have influenced who you are as a sexual being.

Worried you will never get past generational trauma around sexuality? Don't worry! Scientists have also found that positive experiences can correct the epigenetic effects of trauma.

So let's dive into where we come from and the messages we've received from conditioning and genetics, and discover a positive experience of sexuality that will not only change our sexual fate, but the fate of future generations.

Your Grandparents/Ancestors

Exercise: What do you know about the sexuality of your grandparents? Write everything you know, imagine, or feel about the sexuality and experiences of both your paternal and maternal grandparents.

Ex: My paternal grandmother was more or less forced to marry a man she didn't love. She was a virgin when she married. I don't think she ever talked about enjoying sex and spoke of it very matter-of-factly. Her first husband had many sexual affairs during their marriage and she gave him four children. She was very modest, and uptight in her body, but affectionate and loving. She was also very Christian and I feel like sex was associated with shame for her. Her second husband spent most of their marriage in a wheelchair, so I imagine there wasn't any sex between them. I feel sad when I think about my grandmother's sex life and how hard it must have been for her.

Paternal Grandmother:

Paternal Grandfather:

<u>Maternal Grandmother:</u>

<u>Maternal Grandfather:</u>

**Now go back over what you wrote and highlight any words
or phrases that stand out to you.**

Your Parents

Exercise: What do you know about the sexuality of your parents? Write everything you know, imagine, remember or feel about the sexuality of your individual parents and the sexual relationship between them.

Ex: My father was raised in a very religious and suppressive sexual environment where it was not okay to be sexual before marriage. He was a virgin when he met my mother and although he wasn't completely in love with her, he married her after graduate school because it was "the right thing to do" and he told me he "didn't want to lose her." He never spoke to me about sexuality, but I remember him shaming me because I was playing with our puppy in his lap and I must have gotten too close to his penis when he said, "What are you doing?" and there was such a tone of disgust that I have never forgotten how it made me feel. I also remember him harassing me about dating boys, and telling me how he would humiliate them when they came by to date me, and I remember feeling very afraid of humiliation and scared of men in general. I never had a boy over my entire teenage life, except one who picked me up for a dance after my father remarried. My sense is that my father has a lot of anger and shame from his relationship with his father, and that got passed down to us kids. My dad eventually left my mom when I was 15 and within less than six months was remarried to a woman from our church.

<u>Father:</u>

<u>Mother:</u>

<u>The sexual relationship between them:</u>

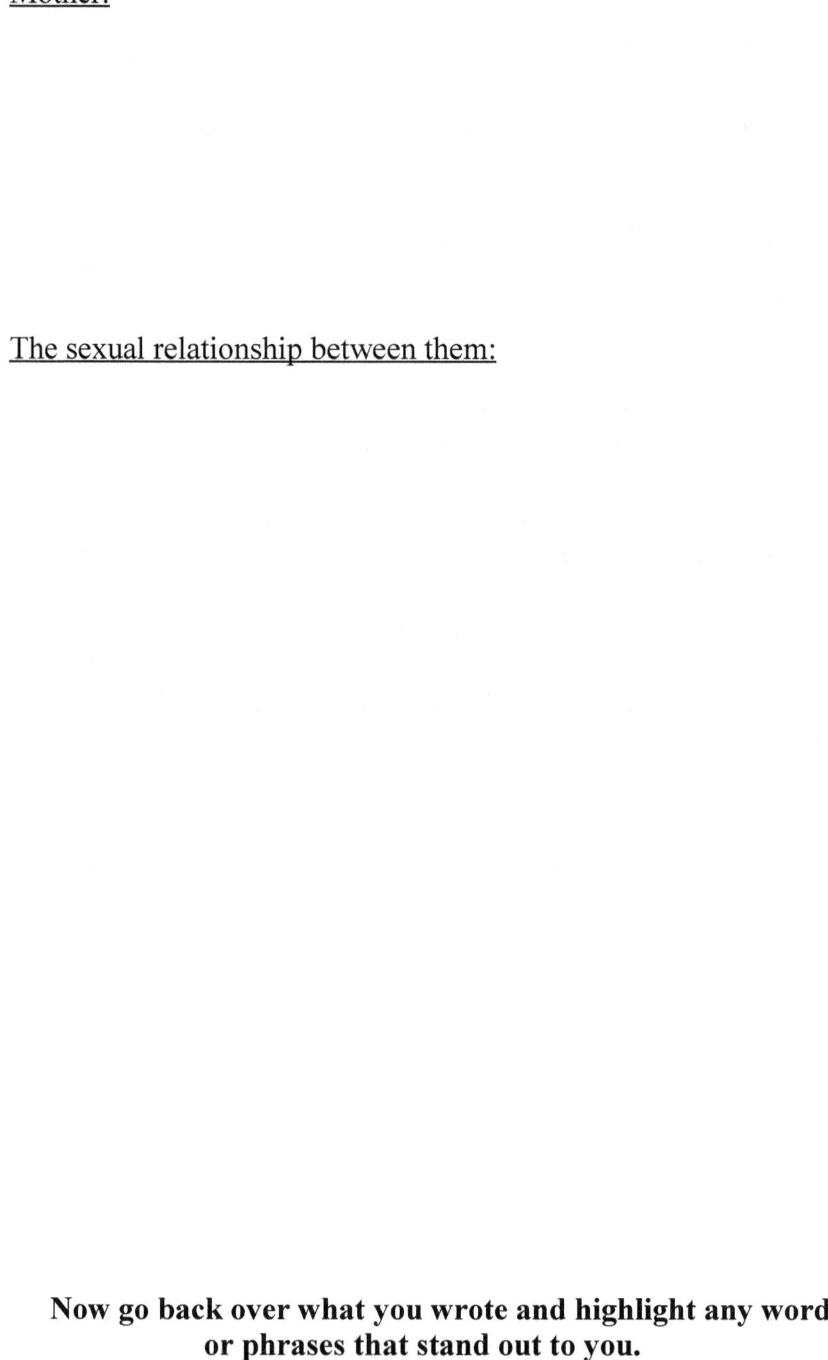

Now go back over what you wrote and highlight any words or phrases that stand out to you.

Your Town/Country

Exercise: What was the general feeling about sexuality where you grew up? What was the relationship to sexuality in that particular decade? What was the societal relationship to nudity, sex before marriage, homosexuality, etc.?

Ex: I grew up in a very conservative Christian town with next to no diversity. Sex belonged in marriage, and I had only one friend with unmarried parents and I could feel as a child that they were "below us" somehow. I didn't learn about homosexuality until I was a teenager and never saw a nude adult except in the women's changing room at the gym with my mother. I was raised in the United States in the 1980s. Sexuality was present but it wasn't talked about, which made it even more shameful. I was very afraid of it.

<u>Your town/city:</u>

<u>Your Country in the (19_0's):</u>

Now go back over what you wrote and highlight any words or phrases that stand out to you.

Chapter 2: What was your sexual education?

In this second chapter we will explore the specifics of our sexual education. What have we learned about sexuality from our friends, caregivers, religious teachers, healthcare providers and other sources of education? After all, it is only in uncovering what we have been taught about sexuality that we can find the origins of our fears and anxieties about it. Much of what we were taught about sexuality is untrue (ex: masturbation is dirty and will make you sick), and yet it has gone unexamined our whole adult lives. This chapter is an opportunity to unearth our sexual education and understand more deeply why we relate to sexuality the way we do.

Education at a young age seeps directly into our subconscious mind and becomes the unconscious way we relate to the world. Growing up believing that sexuality is dangerous or wrong can have profound effects on our life, not only as a child, but in our adult sexual relationships. This is because those unexamined belief systems cause our nervous system to react as though there is danger present even if we consciously feel safe. For example, we might feel excited about a new relationship, and even more excited to have sex, but if our genitals are not responding appropriately, such as with a lack of lubrication, a tight vaginal opening, or the lack of an erection, this is often due to unconscious fears about sex itself. As we unravel what is influencing our subconscious mind in the realm of sex, our nervous system will react the way it is designed to in our sexual encounters, viewing them as safe and exciting. The work in this chapter will affect not only our basic sexual anatomy and physiology, but our ability to have more pleasure with sex, improve our overall sexual health, and deepen the intimacy in our relationships.

Religious Institutions

Exercise: Write out everything you can remember learning about sexuality from your church or religion. This can include religious or spiritual ideas you received from family members, religious peers and their families, or institutions that taught or supported religious ideas about sexuality such as schools or clubs. Additionally, what cultural or religious ideas were disseminated to you by magazines, newspapers, movies, audios or other sources. Try to include both specific memories you have, as well as stories that have been recounted to you about your own life.

Ex: We grew up attending church every Sunday, singing in the choir when I was young, and attending vacation Bible study in the summer. My parents were very religious, and my father would read the Bible by himself at home when we didn't attend church. I can't remember specific teachings at church but I knew that sex was for marriage, marriage was sacred to God, and divorce was sinful. I was also raised that God and Jesus were compassionate and forgiving, but I don't know if this applied to sexuality. But while I was raised to obey, I was also raised to question, and my father embodied that questioning and independent thinking in always asking us children what we though of sermons, and in sharing his own disagreements with what the pastor said during the Sunday sermon. We changed churches a lot, because my father was always in search of a minister whose teachings he agreed with. I can't remember the specifics of what was taught to me in the teenage ministry during high school, but I remember it being reinforced that sexuality had to be controlled and resisted until marriage, and that about the worst thing that could happen to you would be to end up unmarried and pregnant. There were never any positive stories about sexuality, only sad stories about teenage pregnancy and shame. I knew I didn't want to be one of those "dumb" women who couldn't control themselves and got pregnant or lost her virginity because she couldn't control herself, and I definitely wanted to wait to have sex until marriage and make everyone proud of me and happy.

<u>What did you learn as a child about sexuality from religion?</u>

<u>What did you learn as a teenager about sexuality from religion?</u>

<u>What religious or spiritual ideas have shaped your sexuality as an adult?</u>

Now go back over what you wrote and highlight any words or phrases that stand out to you.

School and Peers

Exercise: What was your sexual education at school, including from peers, teachers, books and sexual ed or physical education classes?

Ex: I remember my sex ed class in the fifth grade like it was yesterday. I don't remember exactly what was taught, but I remember hearing the word 'penis' and 'vagina' used publicly and an overwhelming and stiffening wave of embarrassment and disgust running through my body. I remember the teacher talking about the changes of puberty, and the idea that my body would have a menstrual cycle and grow breasts and one day engage in sex and it was terrifying and nauseating. I had a best friend that was boy-crazy that year and would kiss this boy on the playground and I remember how scared I was of boys and how unready I was to kiss one. The whole experience made me feel babyish, afraid, immature, and like something was wrong with me. I guess the overwhelming feeling was that something was wrong with me. Why was I so afraid of that stuff?

<u>What was your sexual education in the classroom?:</u>

**Now go back over what you wrote and highlight any words
or phrases that stand out to you.**

Babysitters and Family Members

Exercise: Write out any memories relating to sexuality with babysitters, family member or other adults.

Ex: I have two strong memories with babysitters. The first was when my sister was still a toddler and our babysitter told her to undress and get in the bathtub. For some reason I freaked out and thought my sister was going to be molested and I wouldn't let my babysitter near my sister that night. I don't remember the specifics of the incident as much as I remember hearing her tell my mother what happened when she came home and I remember feeling confusion and shame. Here I had saved my sister from sexual molestation, or did I? I knew was in trouble. The funny thing is we regularly had that babysitter, so I don't know what triggered the sudden fear that my sister would be molested by her if she was naked. The second memory was when these two teenagers where babysitting us at a friend's house. I remember the feeling that they were having sex, and when I saw a brown stain on her white jeans I remember thinking, "Oh my God, they are having sex because she has that poop stain on her jeans." Sex to me was clearly dirty and connected to the anus.

<u>What are your memories of sexuality with babysitters?:</u>

What are your memories of sexuality with other adults in your life including family members, friends of your parents, people in the community, neighbors, or adults connected to your peers?:

Now go back over what you wrote and highlight any words or phrases that stand out to you.

Chapter 3: What did your sexual relationships teach you?

In this chapter we will explore what we learned from our sexual relationships. All of our romantic and sexual relationships bring both blessings and challenges. While they teach us incredible things about our own sexuality, there can often be things done or said by a lover that scar us for life. Most people never dare to share what went on sexually in their relationships because it feels like it will only amplify the shame they felt then and are still feeling now. However, when we find the courage to examine the experiences in our past relationships and bring them into the light, those dark scars can heal and become simply faint memories.

Often what someone is shamed by sexually can be remedied through sexual education. If this is the case, I recommend reading the full book, *The New Rules of Sex* to develop a better understanding of the huge range of normal sexual experiences, desires and practices that exist as a part of human sexuality. We are all normal! And we must learn to embrace our sexuality with education, conversation, and a playful, curious attitude, as we continue discover new things about sexuality with every sexual experience. Like life, sexuality is a journey from birth until death, and so no matter our age, we have lots of time to continue exploring! Sex, like wine, gets better as we age, in fact, and deepening our knowledge and self-acceptance is the most important place to begin.

Self-acceptance and love of our bodies and sexuality increases as we review the hang-ups we've developed throughout our life's journey. Is there something that was said or done to us that we haven't let go of? Has someone's comment, or maybe what they didn't say, shaped how we feel about ourself as a sexual being? This chapter will help identify hangups around sex or body image from relationships, beginning with experiences we had as a child or teen, and continuing up to our current adult relationships. The space between two people is deeply intimate and vulnerable, and where we are open to grow the most in life, is also where we are most vulnerable. So let's dive into those intimate moments and take a fresh look at where shame or fear is holding us back from a fantastic, fun and liberated experience of sex and sexuality in all of our intimate relationships.

Childhood Relationships

Exercise: Think back to your early sexual, romantic or other types of relationships that took place in childhood and had some impact on how you viewed sex, relationships or your body.

Ex: I remember when I was maybe seven years old and my parents had a Christmas party and had all of their friends and their kids over. I took the girls into my room and we started playing dress up and trying on different vintage dresses I had in my room. We later found out that my brother and the boys had gone outside and been spying on us through the window of my bedroom. I felt sick (and still feel sick now) thinking about the fact that they all saw my chest and nipples as I was changing from dress to dress in only my underwear. I felt sad, angry, betrayed, abused and violated and I never let go of the shame I felt at that moment as I was violated by the boys I had known and grown up with. It was a horrible feeling. I can still feel it in my chest now, like I want to suck my breasts into my body so they can't be seen, desired or touched by anyone. I want them to be invisible. I need to let go of that anger. They were only boys and weren't really hurting me in any way. And why was I such a prude about nudity anyway? Who cares if someone sees my boobs- they're just boobs! The experience really left me with a feeling of shame and sadness.

Describe any memories (listing them separately) that you have with your parents, siblings or other family members from childhood that felt sexual or impacted how you felt about your sexuality or body:

List any memories having to do with touching yourself,
masturbation, sexual dreams, exploration or desire where you
were caught or confronted:

What do you need to let go of regarding your childhood
experience of sexuality?

**Now go back over what you wrote and highlight any words or
phrases that stand out to you.**

Teenage Relationships

Exercise: Think back to your early sexual, romantic or other types of relationships that took place in your teenage years and had some impact on how you viewed sex, relationships or your body.

Ex: When I think back on my teenage relationships I see how scared, terrified really, I was off sexuality or intimacy with men. There were very few men I felt safe enough to kiss, and they were only utterly unavailable men with no real feelings for me. The ones that liked me scared the shit out of me, and I would proceed to get so drunk I would pass out so that I could either avoid them or go through with sexuality unconsciously. Looking back I had a terrible relationship with my dad and felt unseen, unloved, uncared for and unimportant, so it makes total sense that I couldn't possibly relate to a loving man at that point in my life. Luckily I am mostly past that now! I feel so bad for teenage Lauren and that things were so hard for her. It didn't help that she was told her whole life not to have sex until marriage, and that even dating was never discusses by anyone, and the whole relationship thing felt uncomfortable and scary. I had all this sexual energy and no guidance about what to do with it. The whole situation with relationships and sex just made me feel even worse about myself than I already felt and made my self-esteem go down the toilet. I had a few friends who were having sex and it seemed so nonchalant and easy for them, which made me really feel like something was wrong with me. But nothing is wrong with me, and although I struggled at that time, I'm grateful I have the relationship to sexuality I have now. I learned about sex the hard way, but I've mastered what many of my friends have never dared to even explore and I am extremely happy with my sexuality now!

Describe any memories (listing them separately) with romantic partners and how they impacted how you felt about sexuality or your body:

List any memories around sexuality relating to parents, adults or other non-romantic partners:

What do you need to let go of regarding your teenage experience of sexual relationships?

Now go back over what you wrote and highlight any words or phrases that stand out to you.

Adult Relationships

Exercise: Think back over your sexual, romantic or other types of relationships from adulthood and how they have impacted your sexuality, focusing on any negativity around sex or your body that developed from those experiences.

Ex: My adult sexual relationships have exposed me to a broad spectrum of sexuality. I've had great sex and horrible sex. I generally feel pretty great about the experiences I have, but I can remember a couple of moments where I did not feel great. Mostly having sex with people I didn't really want to have sex with, or having a lot of non-sexual intimacy with someone and then having them end the relationship and feeling used and lied to. I do remember sleeping with this older guy who was really just a rebound after my heart had been completely shattered into a million pieces. I was open to attention from just about anyone and this guy had an easy time seducing me. I didn't enjoy the sex much, but I liked almost everything else about being with him. However I'll never forget how he acted when I was on my period, mainly his disgust and refusal to have sex with me, and how he'd look at my shaved pubic hair and say it was too prickly, offering to shave it for me, declaring he was supposedly able to do a better job. There was something about how he interacted with me about those things that made me feel not good enough. But I guess it's no surprise as I had felt absolutely "good enough" when my boyfriend prior to him broke up with me without any warning. That was a sad time in life and my sexuality, but I am truly grateful that man was there to provide some tenderness and love when I was so broken hearted. In the end, I was the one to break it off with him and now I am grateful for the experience and what I learned from him. Imagine if he was my only lover! I would have such a warped view of sex with men!

Describe any memories (listing them separately) that you have with casual or serious sexual relationships that impacted how you felt about your sexuality or body:

List any memories you've had with other adults, such as healthcare providers, religious figures, friends, or others who have shamed you, judged you, or made you feel you weren't okay:

What do you need to let go of regarding your adult experience of sexuality?:

Now go back over what you wrote and highlight any words or phrases that stand out to you.

Chapter 4: What are your belief systems about sexuality and relationships?

Buried deep within the sexual programing from our family, culture, religion, education and relationships are belief systems that influence how we think, perceive and respond to the sexuality and sexual experiences of ourselves and others. Belief systems are present that may only be seen once we are thrust into a particular situation, like when we encounter something new sexually, become pregnant or have children, start to experience aging, or encounter someone whose sexual mores are different than our own, but they have been there from the beginning of our lives, buried in our subconscious. This chapter seeks to uncover what those beliefs are so that we can examine them and start to open up more flexibility and freedom in how we relate to our body, our sexuality and the sexuality of others. This investigation into how we've been taught to think and feel can catalyze a revolution in how we relate to sexuality, and can even create a dramatic change of physiology and function.

Belief systems also deeply impact our relationships. The human brain is set up to see, hear, smell, taste and feel what it has felt before. When new information enters the brain via the sensory organs, that new information is combined with information from the past to create your current experience of "reality." What you think you are experiencing is actually 80 to 90 percent memory combined with 10 to 20 percent new data. This is why you sometimes do a double take when you think you see something spelled correctly, only to discover that it was spelled incorrectly but your brain filled in the correct spelling. So this is partly why our past, and the belief systems we formed from those experiences, follows us through life influencing our present experience. We live in a perpetual groundhog day until we come to consciousness about what we are creating. So how to we escape from experiencing the same reality over and over again? We must get to the source of the past experience and challenge the information that tells us how things should be. When did you form the belief system that you were unloveable? Or bad at sex? Or that girls didn't like you? Even though this investigation can be painful, the good news is that our brains and minds have enormous plasticity, or potential for change, and we can experience sex and relationships in new ways. We just have to change our operating system when it comes to sex.

Sex as dirty, sinful and shameful

Exercise: List times in your life where you felt dirty, sinful and shameful about sex. Then list all the reasons sex is not dirty, sinful or shameful and include memories of sexuality that supported that experience.

Ex: I felt really dirty and sinful about sex when I was at the gynecologist's office and she told me I had three very small genital warts. I was so ashamed that she was looking at my genitals and finding something that I considered gross. I felt diseased, and I wondered if she though I was having sex with "too many people" or the wrong people. It was so hard to hear her say the words out loud, but at the same time, I was grateful it wasn't something worse, and grateful she could burn them off right there before I left the office. Goodbye, warts. I was a little scared of the pain, but knew instinctively when I saw the first small bump a few months before that it would need to be cut off. It was just HPV, after all, the virus that every single sexually active person has, in the same way that we all have the Chicken Pox virus and tons of other viruses living inside of us. We are made up of more microbes – virus, bacteria, parasite, fungi – than we have human cells, I know. But still, I felt really dirty in the office that day. I also felt dirty the time that I had chlamydia, and all the various times I had an imbalance of yeast or bacteria, or even just a pimple from an ingrown hair. I also remember feeling dirty and shameful when I had sex in my twenties with these two guys I wasn't attracted to. I was in love with my boyfriend who had taken off to Florida even though I asked him not to, to buy a car and meet me in LA. I found out he cheated on me after he left, and my response was to have sex with the next two guys who showed me the slightest bit of attention. I was disgusted with their bodies and disgusted with myself, and the experience haunts me to this day. Though I can have compassion with myself because I know I was hurting and lost and didn't know what to do. I also hadn't had many experiences with men, so I think I was also wanting to see what else was out there. Turns out it wasn't that great. But it takes the bad experiences to let you see how great the good ones are, and how important it is

*to not just say yes to sex unless you really really want it. And I
have had so many great ones where sex felt like the most natural,
loving, human expression of my body and soul. Still, it's hard to
feel 100 percent great about sex in a culture that considers it
wrong.*

List times in your life where you felt dirty, sinful and shameful
about sex:

List all the reasons floating around your unconscious that say sex
is dirty, sinful or shameful:

<u>List all the reasons that sex is *not* dirty, sinful or shameful:</u>

<u>List positive memories of sexuality that showed you that sexuality
is not dirty or shameful:</u>

**Now go back over what you wrote and highlight any words or
phrases that stand out to you.**

Your Body and Body Image

Exercise: Scan through your life and revisit every memory where you were made to feel bad about your body or genitals, touching or pleasuring your body or genitals, or anything else that made you feel like you weren't lovable as you were.

Ex: I think I am pretty fortunate to have a good relationship with my body because I don't remember anyone shaming me about my body, and I was never caught masturbating or playing sex games, so there was no big trauma there. I do remember my dad catching me staring into my eyeball in the mirror and being shamed, maybe for admiring myself, and that experience really lingered with me that it wasn't okay to find myself beautiful. But I've still liked myself and found myself beautiful, despite finding things in myself I wish were different or better. Lovable? I don't know that I ever felt totally lovable. I think feeling lovable or being lovable was dependent on me obeying and being "good." I wasn't ever lovable as I was, and this has been a hard thing to get over in my adult life, because my parents think they love me as I am, but they don't realize that that message never came across in their words or actions. My body though, I enjoy it for the most part. I'm a little insecure of how the skin of my breasts and belly have changed after having a baby, but when I stand up straight, I still like them a lot. I'm grateful for that.

<u>List every memory where you were made to feel bad about your body or genitals:</u>

<u>List any memories where something or someone made you feel unloveable:</u>

Now go back over what you wrote and highlight any words or phrases that stand out to you.

Beliefs about Sex

Exercise: Respond to the statements below with a yes/no, and then elaborate on any memories associated with that particular belief system or experience.

<u>You can be sexual with any consenting adult partner you desire:</u>

<u>You don't have to wait for marriage or commitment to have sex, or withhold sex to manipulate a partner:</u>

<u>Sexuality is normal and healthy:</u>

<u>Sexuality is pleasurable:</u>

<u>Sexuality is empowering:</u>

<u>Humans are sexual beings from birth until death:</u>

Sexuality can lead to a pregnancy unless forms of birth control or family planning are utilized:

Sexuality is used for purposes other than procreation, such as strengthening social bonds, relaxation, repair in relationships, and improving general wellbeing:

Women and men are multi-orgasmic:

Women must be turned on before penetration takes place, as their arousal generates lubrication of the vagina and vulva:

Men often fail to achieve an erection or lose their erection during sex due to emotions and fears:

Men enjoy sex even when they don't ejaculate:

Men can learn to have orgasms without ejaculating:

Men enjoy being penetrated and general anal play:

Women are capable of orgasms in their external clitoris, internal vagina, cervix, rectum, anus, nipples, full body orgasms, and many more locations:

Giving birth is a sexual experience and birth proceeds best when a woman feels safe and is free to be sensual and sexual:

All forms of sexuality are natural and pleasurable including manual, oral, vaginal, and anal sex:

Sexual expression is normal and healthy between same-sex partners, solo, coupled or with multiple partners:

When others judge or condemn my sexuality it's because they have their own shame and conditioning around sex that makes them unable to embrace who they truly are sexually:

Beliefs about Relationships

Exercise: Respond to the false statements below with a yes/no, and then elaborate on any memories associated with that particular belief system or experience.

Ex: Yes. I remember feeling fear when I was young that men would shame me if they knew I had no sexual experience, and years later I felt fear that men would shame me for having what they deemed "too much" sexual experience. What was enough? It was silly, I know, to hold myself to this idea of "just the right amount of sexual experience." You have what you have. And the right person appreciates your past because it makes you who you are. Still, I think it's hard to get past a society that shames you for sex. You feel it even when you're not thinking about it. It's just always there.

No one will want me if I don't have a lot of sexual experience:

If I've had too much sex they will think I'm a slut:

If you have sex too soon you ruin the relationship and they think you're easy:

Sex eventually fades in relationships and becomes boring:

It's the men that always want sex:

Sexual monogamy is the only way to proceed in a healthy relationship:

You can't have sex when you're older because things stop working:

You won't want sex anymore after you (or your partner) have had a baby:

Women use sex to manipulate men:

No one can be sexually faithful:

It's not okay to ask for what I want sexually:

It's not okay if my partner and I have different ideas about what is sexy:

It's impossible to meet your partner's sexual needs while also staying true to how you feel:

Sex on your period is dirty:

Sex is not okay when the kids are around:

I'm not safe if my partner finds someone else attractive:

I'm not turned on by my partner because I'm just not that sexual:

Sex in longterm relationships just gets better and better:

Chapter 5: What do you truly desire?

In every culture we are limited in our ability to explore what we truly desire because societal rules and taboos. They tell us what is acceptable and unacceptable, shameful or honorable, saintly or deviant in our sexual relationships and experiences, and because we don't want to be labeled bad, found to be unloveable, or cast out from the tribe, we strive to not only follow these guidelines, but internalize them as if they were our own personal preferences. For this reason, one can suppress who they truly are for decades, and some never discover what lies beneath the layers and layers of suppression of things that have been innate from the very beginning of their lives. Even when one is able to confront the true nature of their sexual desire and the suppression that has kept it hidden, they often struggle not to feel shame, grief, isolation or self-pity, including physical manifestations of these emotions as pain or disease, until they find others like them and do some deep healing work to truly accept who they are.

So what do you truly desire? Who are you as a sexual being? What have you been exploring since someone first told you what was good and bad, right and wrong, and acceptable or unacceptable. Are you ready to re-write some of those rules? Let's explore concepts such as freedom, equality, orientation, and sexual palate to explore the full range of human sexuality. It is only in exploration that we can discover what might bring the greatest satisfaction, authenticity and happiness in our individual sexual expression.

Freedom and Equality in Sexuality

Exercise: Respond to the statements below with a yes/no based on whether or not the statement is true in your life right now, and then elaborate on the vision you have for what the greatest expression of that statement might look like for you personally.

Ex: Yes. I am definitely free to be myself in my relationships. The only thing I continue to experience is being with partners that are defensive, and this makes me feel like my voice isn't heard, and my feelings don't matter. This makes me sad, and I eventually leave these relationships. I am not defensive, so I know I can find someone who can also take responsibility and really hear what I need. My father was usually defensive, so I'm sure that somehow feels like love to me, but I envision a relationship where defensiveness is not a part of it and I feel free to be myself without changing who I am to avoid my partner's reaction.

I am free to be myself in my relationship(s):

I am free to be who I am sexually in my relationship(s):

My relationship(s) supports my sexual expression:

I am free to masturbate, communicate desire, and initiate sex with my partner(s):

I regularly experience pleasure and achieve orgasm easily in relationship(s):

I am free to be naked and allow wild sexual energy to flow through my body:

I am free to talk about sex with friends, health care practitioners, partners and my children:

My partner(s) and I are treated equally in the relationship and share the workloads equally:

My partner and I have equal sexual pleasure:

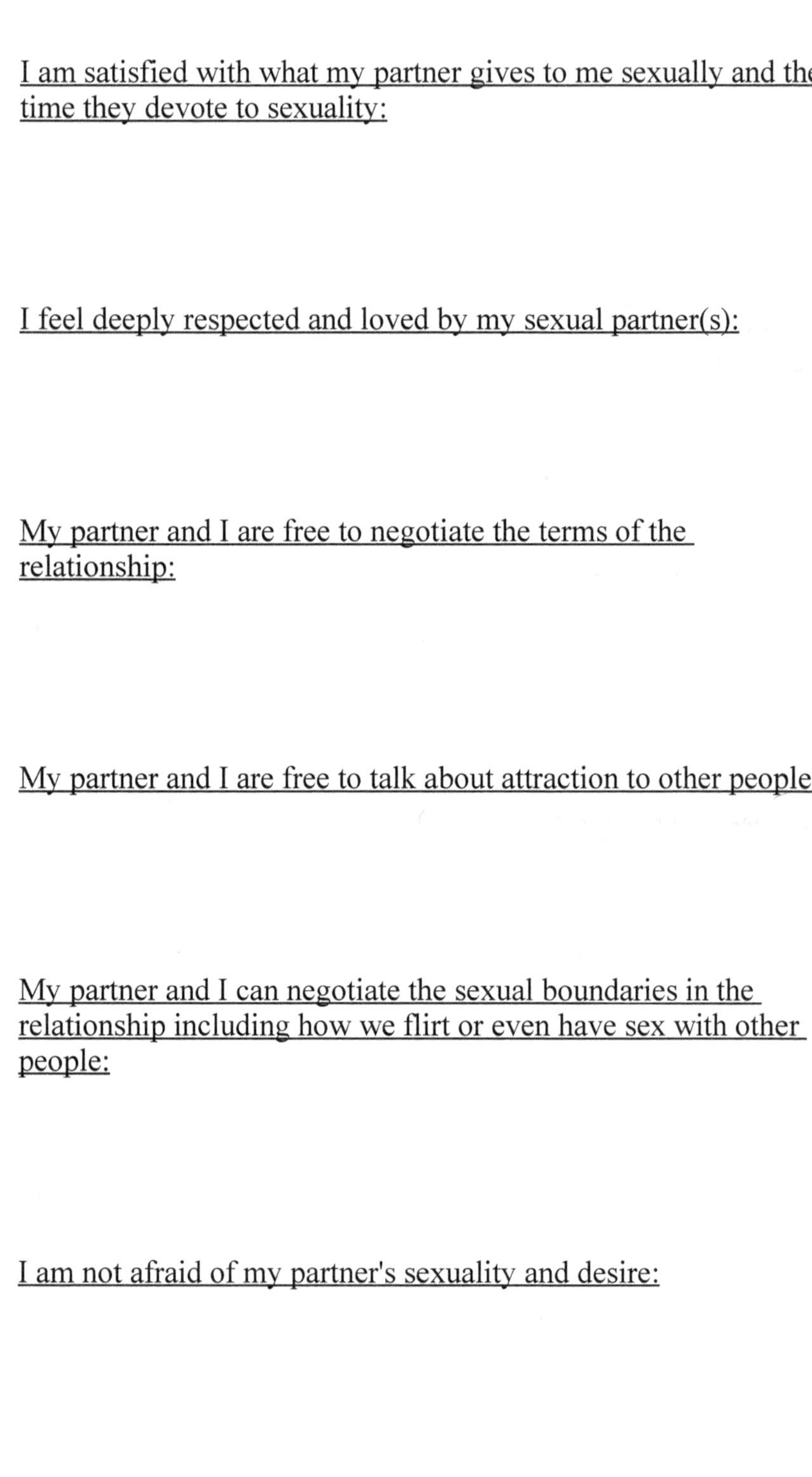

<u>I am satisfied with what my partner gives to me sexually and the time they devote to sexuality:</u>

<u>I feel deeply respected and loved by my sexual partner(s):</u>

<u>My partner and I are free to negotiate the terms of the relationship:</u>

<u>My partner and I are free to talk about attraction to other people:</u>

<u>My partner and I can negotiate the sexual boundaries in the relationship including how we flirt or even have sex with other people:</u>

<u>I am not afraid of my partner's sexuality and desire:</u>

Sexual Orientation and your Sexual Palate

Exercise: Respond to the statements below with a yes/no based on whether or not the statement is true in your life right now, and then elaborate on the vision you have for what the greatest expression of that statement might look like for you personally.

Ex: Yes. I have been wildly attracted to a gay man since I was in high school, and we are still friends today. I will always be in love with him. So that is a perfect example. I have been attracted to straight, bi and even very masculine gay women, but only in recent years when something finally opened up in me to that. I wasn't turned on by masculine women until then, and now I find them extremely attractive. I met the first trans person that I was attracted to a couple of years ago and that was a really beautiful experience that opened me up even more. They were almost neither man nor woman to me, and I felt how I was just attracted to their being, not even knowing how to label them in my mind, so that was really life changing for me. I'm also very much attracted to heterosexual and bisexual men. What does someone do when they are attracted to every sexual orientation??? I guess just own it and see where it takes me!

I find myself attracted to people as suppose to any specific gender or orientation:

I am completely comfortable with any expression of sexual orientation in my environment including same-sex couples, trans people, and both heterosexual and homosexual couples of varying different ages, incomes, races or any other factor:

I am comfortable with different formats for relationships including those who choose to marry, remain unmarried, have multiple relationships at one time, casual sex, varying degrees of openness in their relationships, children or no children, become swingers, or engage in kink, or any other form of traditional or non-traditional relationship:

I experience a wide range of sexual fantasies:

I am able to get aroused by a wide range of sexual energies and activities from very loving or sensual to animalistic or kinky:

I have a wide sexual palate and don't need one particular thing to turn me on:

I'm continually discovering new things about my sexuality:

Going Beyond your Comfort Zone

Exercise: Respond to the questions below after taking time to check in with yourself about what is really true for you.

Ex: To let go even more in my sexuality I need a partner who can hold space for my woman to come out, for my masculine to come out, for my dominant to come out, and who can make me feel so safe and cared for and dominated that my true submissive can come out. I need a partner I love and feel loved by with every cell of my body, and who I can grow deeper into intimacy with each and every day. I need to know they will never abandon me, even if they find themselves sexually attracted to others. I also need to be able to have the time, space and privacy to have loud sex!

<u>What do you need to let go even more in your sexual experiences?:</u>

<u>What do you need to feel even better in and about your body?:</u>

<u>What do you need to feel safe to experience more intimacy, honesty and vulnerability in your relationship(s)?:</u>

<u>What do you need to give yourself to have permission to be the most authentic and honest version of your sexual self?:</u>

What's the scariest thing about sexuality for you and how can you face it?:

What's one thing you could do this week that would take you beyond your sexual comfort zone and into unexplored terrain?:

What would thrill you sexually more than anything else?

What's something you are triggered by in another that is really something you desire for yourself?

What are you jealous of in another person's sexual experience, and how can you create that experience for yourself?:

Sexual Happiness and Satisfaction

Exercise: Respond to the questions below after taking time to check in with yourself about what is really true for you, and come up with a plan and a vision going forward for your sexual happiness and satisfaction.

Ex: I have always dreamed of being a sex worker but I have never done it. Writing my thesis made me want to explore it even more. When you enjoy sex a lot, the thought of getting paid to do something you love seems too good to be true! Will have to look into that more. Every job, no matter how seemingly glamorous has it's down sides. For the time being it can just be a fantasy, I guess!

<u>What have you always dreamed of doing sexually but have never done?:</u>

<u>What is the one sexual fantasy you have never realized?:</u>

<u>What would increase your sexual happiness today and over the next five years?</u>

What conversation do you need to have with your partner(s) to have more sexual pleasure and satisfaction?:

How are you sabotaging your sexuality?:

Where are you still carrying sexual shame in your life or body?:

What unrealized potential is still latent in your sexual body?:

Where could there be more pleasure and satisfaction in your sexuality going forward?

Re-writing the Rules of Sex

Final Exercise: Detail how you would like to proceed with your sexuality after everything you've discovered about yourself on this journey? What goals do you have? What have you realized about yourself? What has opened up for you in your understanding of who you are as a sexual being? What's next for you?

Ex: I've discovered that I ...... I want to have more ..... I realize I can let go of the idea that..... I'm going to pursue ....

Closing Remarks

 It has been such a pleasure taking this journey with you! I hope that you have discovered many new things about your sexuality that were previously hidden from view, had never been questioned, or were buried in shame or secrecy. Now that everything's out in the light, it's not so scary, right? You are a beautiful, healthy, sexual being and you deserve happiness and satisfaction in your sexual relationships. We are all on a sexual journey with no real beginning or ending, but with plenty of learning and discovery along the way. The fact that you devoted the time that you did to this workbook means that your sexuality is important to you, and that is a critical first step in developing a deeply loving and respectful relationship with your whole self. Don't forget it was sex that created you, so sex must be important! Our society has dismissed the importance of sex, but it's the sexual and reproduction energy of your cells that is keeping you alive and healthy as you read these words. So go enjoy your newly discovered sexuality and stay true to what you've learned about yourself. And be ready for things to keep changing! Because our sexuality is always evolving if we stay open minded in our exploration. Stay curious, stay open, and keep loving your special uniqueness. The more we love ourselves *just* the way we are, the more we support a culture that does the same. So thank you for your contribution to a better, more peaceful world through your conscious sexual exploration. You are amazing.

To your fantastic, fulfilling sex life!

- Lauren Brim, Doctor of Human Sexuality